EDGARDO FERNANDEZ CLIMENT

Mastering NIST SP 800-53

A Small Business IT Professional's Roadmap to Compliance

To my dearest Graciela, your unwavering support, boundless love, and enduring encouragement have been the guiding lights that fueled the creation of this book. Your belief in my endeavors has been my greatest motivation.

Thank you for being the anchor in the storm, the muse of my creativity, and the constant source of inspiration. With all my love, this book is dedicated to you, Graciela.

Contents

Chapter 1: Introduction to NIST SP 800-53 Compliance

Understanding the Importance of NIST SP 800-53 Compliance for Small Businesses

As an IT professional working in a small business, you may be wondering about the relevance and significance of NIST SP 800-53 compliance for your organization. In this section, we will delve into the key reasons why small businesses should prioritize NIST SP 800-53 compliance and the benefits it can bring to their operations.

NIST SP 800-53, also known as the "Security and Privacy Controls for Federal Information Systems and Organizations," is a comprehensive set of guidelines and controls developed by the National Institute of Standards and Technology (NIST) to ensure the security and privacy of sensitive government information. While initially intended for federal agencies, NIST SP 800-53 has become increasingly important for businesses of all sizes, including small businesses, due to the growing threat landscape and regulatory requirements.

One of the primary reasons small businesses should focus on NIST SP

800-53 compliance is the need to safeguard sensitive data. Small businesses are not immune to cyber threats, and the potential consequences of a data breach can be devastating. By implementing the controls and best practices outlined in NIST SP 800-53, you can enhance your organization's overall security posture, mitigate risks, and protect your valuable data from unauthorized access, theft, or compromise.

Moreover, NIST SP 800-53 compliance demonstrates your commitment to security and privacy, which can have a positive impact on your business reputation. Customers, partners, and stakeholders are increasingly concerned about data security, and compliance with industry standards such as NIST SP 800-53 can differentiate your small business from competitors and instill trust in your ability to handle sensitive information.

Furthermore, NIST SP 800-53 compliance can help small businesses align with legal and regulatory requirements. Many industries, such as healthcare, finance, and government contracting, have specific security and privacy regulations that small businesses must adhere to. By implementing the controls outlined in NIST SP 800-53, you can ensure that your small business meets the necessary compliance obligations and avoid costly penalties or legal consequences.

Lastly, NIST SP 800-53 compliance provides a framework for continuous improvement and proactive risk management. The controls and guidelines outlined in NIST SP 800-53 are designed to be flexible and scalable, allowing small businesses to tailor their security programs to their unique needs and resources. By following this framework, small businesses can identify vulnerabilities, implement necessary safeguards, and continuously evaluate and improve their security posture to stay ahead of emerging threats.

In conclusion, NIST SP 800-53 compliance is a critical consideration for small businesses. It helps protect sensitive data, enhance business reputation, meet legal and regulatory requirements, and foster a culture of continuous improvement. By mastering NIST SP 800-53, you can navigate the complex world of cybersecurity and position your small business for long-term success in today's digital landscape.

Overview of NIST SP 800-53 and its Relevance in the IT Industry

NIST SP 800-53, also known as the National Institute of Standards and Technology Special Publication 800-53, is a comprehensive set of guidelines and controls designed to enhance the security of information systems within the federal government. It provides a framework for managing and mitigating risks associated with information security, and its implementation has become increasingly important in the IT industry.

In today's digital era, where cyber threats are constantly evolving and becoming more sophisticated, IT professionals must have a solid understanding of NIST SP 800-53 and its relevance to their organizations. This section aims to overview this important standard and highlight its significance in the IT industry.

NIST SP 800-53 is not limited to federal agencies; it has gained recognition as a leading security framework and is widely adopted by organizations across various sectors, including small businesses. Its implementation is particularly relevant for small businesses as they often lack the resources and expertise to develop and maintain robust security measures. By following the guidelines outlined in NIST SP

800-53, small businesses can effectively manage risks, protect sensitive information, and ensure compliance with industry regulations.

The framework consists of a comprehensive set of security controls categorized into 18 families, covering various aspects of information security such as access control, incident response, and system and information integrity. These controls are designed to address specific risks and provide a structured approach to safeguarding information systems.

Implementing NIST SP 800-53 can offer several benefits to IT professionals and their organizations. It provides a standardized approach to security management, ensuring consistency and interoperability between different systems and networks. It also helps organizations align their security practices with industry best practices and regulatory requirements, enhancing their overall security posture.

Furthermore, NIST SP 800-53 promotes a risk-based approach to security, allowing organizations to prioritize their efforts and allocate resources effectively. This helps IT professionals identify and mitigate potential vulnerabilities, reducing the likelihood of security incidents and their associated impacts.

In conclusion, NIST SP 800-53 is a critical standard that IT professionals should be well-versed in, especially those working in small businesses. Its implementation can significantly enhance the security posture of organizations, mitigate risks, and ensure compliance with industry regulations. By following the guidelines outlined in NIST SP 800-53, IT professionals can establish a strong foundation for information security and protect their organizations from evolving cyber threats.

Benefits of Achieving NIST SP 800-53 Compliance for Small Business IT Professionals

In today's digital landscape, cybersecurity has become a top priority for organizations of all sizes. Small businesses, in particular, are increasingly targeted by cybercriminals due to their limited resources and often inadequate security measures. To safeguard their sensitive data, small business IT professionals must consider implementing the National Institute of Standards and Technology (NIST) Special Publication (SP) 800-53 compliance framework. This section explores the numerous benefits that come with achieving NIST SP 800-53 compliance for small business IT professionals.

1. Enhanced Data Security:

NIST SP 800-53 compliance provides small businesses with a comprehensive framework for developing and maintaining an effective cybersecurity program. By adhering to this standard, IT professionals can implement robust security controls and best practices, ensuring the confidentiality, integrity, and availability of their organization's sensitive information.

2. Regulatory Compliance:

NIST SP 800-53 compliance also helps small businesses meet various regulatory requirements. Many industries have specific cybersecurity regulations in place, and by achieving NIST SP 800-53 compliance, IT professionals can ensure that their organization remains in line with these regulations, avoiding potential penalties and legal consequences.

3. Increased Customer Trust:

Data breaches and cyberattacks can severely damage a small business's reputation. By demonstrating their commitment to data security through NIST SP 800-53 compliance, IT professionals can instill confidence in their customers and partners, fostering trust and potentially attracting new business opportunities.

4. Improved Incident Response:

NIST SP 800-53 compliance emphasizes the importance of incident response planning. Small business IT professionals who follow this framework can develop effective incident response procedures, enabling them to detect, respond to, and recover from cybersecurity incidents more efficiently and effectively.

5. Cost Savings:

While the initial investment in achieving NIST SP 800-53 compliance may seem daunting, it can lead to long-term cost savings. By implementing robust security measures, small businesses can significantly reduce the risk of costly data breaches, legal battles, and reputational damage. Moreover, compliance can also help organizations negotiate lower cyber insurance premiums, further reducing financial risk.

6. Competitive Advantage:

In an increasingly competitive market, small businesses that can demonstrate their commitment to cybersecurity through NIST SP 800-53 compliance gain a competitive edge. By differentiating themselves as secure and trustworthy partners, they can attract more clients and stand out from their competitors.

In conclusion, achieving NIST SP 800-53 compliance offers numerous benefits for small business IT professionals. From enhanced data security to regulatory compliance, increased customer trust, improved incident response, cost savings, and a competitive advantage, complying with this standard can help IT professionals navigate the complex cybersecurity landscape and protect their organizations from evolving threats. By following the roadmap provided in this book, small business IT professionals can successfully implement NIST SP 800-53 and ensure the long-term security and success of their organization.

Chapter 2: NIST SP 800-53 Framework Overview

Understanding the NIST SP 800-53 Framework and its Components

The NIST SP 800-53 framework is a comprehensive set of guidelines and controls that helps organizations protect their information systems and data from various security threats. It is primarily designed for federal agencies but can also be adopted by small businesses to ensure compliance with industry standards and best practices. In this section, we will delve into the various components of the NIST SP 800-53 framework and how they can be implemented effectively by IT professionals in small businesses.

The first component of the framework is the control catalog, which consists of a comprehensive list of security controls categorized into 18 families. These controls cover various aspects of information security, including access control, incident response, system and information integrity, and risk assessment. IT professionals need to understand these controls thoroughly to assess their relevance and applicability to their organization's specific needs.

Next, we have the control baselines, which are predefined sets of controls tailored for different types of information systems. These baselines provide a starting point for small businesses to develop their security posture. IT professionals can use these baselines as a guide to determine which controls are necessary for their organization's systems and customize them accordingly.

Another important component is the assessment procedures, which outline the steps to evaluate the effectiveness of implemented controls. IT professionals need to be familiar with these procedures to conduct regular assessments and identify any vulnerabilities or weaknesses in their organization's security measures. These assessments can help in prioritizing and addressing potential risks efficiently.

The continuous monitoring component emphasizes the need for ongoing monitoring and evaluation of security controls. IT professionals should establish a robust monitoring system that tracks security events, detects anomalies, and alerts relevant personnel. This ensures timely response to security incidents and reduces the overall risk exposure.

Finally, the framework also emphasizes the importance of documenta-tion and security planning. IT professionals should maintain detailed records of security policies, procedures, and control implementations. These documents serve as a reference for future audits and help demon-strate compliance with the framework's requirements.

By understanding these components and implementing them effectively, IT professionals in small businesses can strengthen their organization's security posture and ensure compliance with the NIST SP 800-53 framework. This not only helps protect sensitive information but also enhances the organization's reputation and builds trust with customers and stakeholders.

Description of each of the 18 control families

1. Access Control (AC):
   - Ensure authorized access to information and systems.
   - Assign unique user accounts.
   - Implement multi-factor authentication for privileged accounts.

2. Security Training and Awareness (AT):
   - Develop and implement a security awareness and training program.
   - Provide security awareness training to employees.
   - Include security training in new employee orientation.

3. Audit and Accountability (AU):
   - Develop and implement an audit and accountability policy.
   - Define auditable events and enable auditing on systems.
   - Review and update audit records regularly.

4. Security Assessment and Authorization (CA):
   - Establish a security assessment and authorization process.
   - Conduct security assessments and authorize systems.
   - Implement continuous monitoring and respond to security control failures.

5. Configuration Management (CM):
   - Develop and implement a configuration management policy.
   - Establish and document baseline configurations.
   - Regularly update and review baseline configurations.

6. Contingency Planning (CP):

- Develop and maintain a contingency plan.
- Conduct contingency planning exercises.
- Ensure the availability of backup systems and data.

7. Identification and Authentication (IA):

- Establish and implement identification and authentication policies.
- Use multi-factor authentication for accessing sensitive information.
- Regularly review and update authentication mechanisms.

8. Incident Response (IR):

- Develop and implement an incident response policy.
- Provide incident response training to employees.
- Test incident response capabilities and update plans accordingly.

9. Maintenance (MA):

- Establish and implement maintenance policies and procedures.
- Regularly update and patch systems.
- Conduct maintenance activities in a secure and controlled manner.

10. Media Protection (MP):

- Establish and implement media protection policies.
- Control access to and use of media.
- Protect information during transportation.

11. Physical and Environmental Protection (PE):

- Implement physical security measures to protect information systems.
- Control access to facilities and secure physical assets.
- Monitor and control environmental conditions.

12. Planning (PL):
- Develop and maintain information security plans.
- Align security plans with organizational goals.
- Regularly review and update security plans.

13. Personnel Security (PS):
- Establish and implement personnel security policies.
- Conduct background checks on employees.
- Provide security awareness training to personnel.

14. Risk Assessment (RA):
- Conduct regular risk assessments.
- Identify and assess risks to information systems.
- Develop and implement risk mitigation strategies.

15. Security Assessment (SA):
- Establish and implement security assessment policies.
- Conduct security assessments of information systems.
- Analyze assessment results and take corrective actions.

16. System and Communications Protection (SC):
- Implement security controls to protect communication channels.
- Monitor and control communication at the system boundaries.
- Use encryption to protect information in transit.

17. System and Information Integrity (SI):
- Implement measures to detect and prevent system and information integrity violations.
- Regularly monitor and respond to security events.
- Conduct regular integrity checks on systems.

18. Program Management (PM):

   - Develop and implement information security programs.

   - Establish and maintain program management policies and procedures.

   - Regularly review and update program management practices.

Exploring the Control Families and Control Objectives

To achieve compliance with NIST SP 800-53, IT professionals must understand the control families and control objectives outlined in the framework. These control families provide a comprehensive list of security controls that need to be implemented to protect sensitive information and ensure the overall security of an organization's IT infrastructure.

The control families in NIST SP 800-53 are organized into 18 groups, each focusing on a specific aspect of information security. These families include access control, audit and accountability, configuration management, contingency planning, identification and authentication, incident response, and many more. Each control family consists of multiple control objectives that further define the specific requirements that need to be met.

Understanding the control families and control objectives is essential for IT professionals working in small businesses that are seeking to implement NIST SP 800-53. By familiarizing themselves with these control families, IT professionals can identify the relevant controls that need to be implemented and ensure compliance with the framework.

For example, the access control family focuses on managing user access to systems and data. The control objectives within this family include enforcing password complexity, implementing multi-factor authentication, and regularly reviewing user access privileges. By implementing these controls, small businesses can reduce the risk of unauthorized access and protect sensitive information from potential breaches.

Similarly, the audit and accountability family emphasizes the importance of monitoring and recording system activity. Control objectives within this family may include generating audit logs, conducting regular audits of system activities, and implementing mechanisms to detect and respond to suspicious behavior. By adhering to these control objectives, small businesses can enhance their ability to detect and mitigate potential security incidents.

Overall, exploring the control families and control objectives in NIST SP 800-53 is crucial for IT professionals aiming to implement the framework in small businesses. By understanding these control families and their associated objectives, IT professionals can effectively design and implement security controls that align with the unique needs and requirements of their organization. This knowledge will not only ensure compliance but also enhance the overall security posture of the small business.

Mapping NIST SP 800-53 to Other Compliance Frameworks

As IT professionals, we understand the importance of compliance when it comes to securing our organization's information systems. One of the most widely recognized compliance frameworks is the National Institute of Standards and Technology (NIST) Special Publication (SP) 800-53. This comprehensive set of security controls provides a roadmap for organizations to protect their sensitive data and ensure the confidentiality, integrity, and availability of their systems.

In this section, we will explore how NIST SP 800-53 can be mapped to other compliance frameworks, specifically those relevant to small businesses. While NIST SP 800-53 is a robust and extensive framework, it may not directly align with other compliance requirements that your organization needs to meet. However, by mapping NIST SP 800-53 controls to other frameworks, you can bridge the gap and achieve compliance across multiple standards.

One common compliance framework that small businesses often encounter is the Payment Card Industry Data Security Standard (PCI DSS). PCI DSS focuses on securing payment card data and preventing credit card fraud. By mapping the relevant NIST SP 800-53 controls to the PCI DSS requirements, small businesses can address both sets of controls simultaneously, saving time and resources.

Another framework that may need to be mapped to NIST SP 800-53 is the Health Insurance Portability and Accountability Act (HIPAA). HIPAA sets standards for the protection of individuals' medical information and covers healthcare providers, insurance companies, and related entities. By aligning NIST SP 800-53 controls with HIPAA requirements, small businesses in the healthcare industry can effectively address both compliance frameworks.

Additionally, small businesses operating in the European Union (EU) may need to comply with the General Data Protection Regulation (GDPR). GDPR focuses on protecting the personal data of EU citizens and imposes strict requirements on data handling and security. By mapping NIST SP 800-53 controls to GDPR requirements, small businesses can demonstrate compliance with both frameworks and ensure the protection of personal data.

Mapping NIST SP 800-53 controls to other compliance frameworks is not a one-size-fits-all approach. It requires a thorough understanding of both sets of controls and the ability to identify commonalities and gaps. However, by leveraging the expertise of IT professionals and utilizing tools and resources designed for this purpose, small businesses can streamline the compliance process and achieve a comprehensive and robust security posture.

In conclusion, mapping NIST SP 800-53 controls to other compliance frameworks is essential for small businesses seeking to meet multiple regulatory requirements. By aligning different frameworks, such as PCI DSS, HIPAA, and GDPR, small businesses can efficiently address various compliance obligations and ensure the security of their information systems. This section will provide guidance and practical tips for IT professionals navigating the complexities of mapping NIST SP 800-53 controls to other compliance frameworks, ultimately helping small businesses achieve a strong and compliant security posture.

Chapter 3: Assessing Small Business IT Infrastructure

Identifying Key IT Assets and Systems

In today's digital era, where information technology (IT) forms the backbone of almost every business operation, IT professionals must understand and identify the key IT assets and systems within their organization. This section will delve into the importance of identifying these assets and systems and provide a comprehensive roadmap for IT professionals in small businesses to implement the National Institute of Standards and Technology (NIST) Special Publication (SP) 800-53 guidelines.

The first step in identifying key IT assets and systems is conducting a thorough inventory assessment. This involves identifying all hardware, software, and data assets that are crucial for the organization's daily operations. By documenting and categorizing these assets, IT professionals can gain a clear understanding of what needs protection and what vulnerabilities may exist.

Furthermore, IT professionals must prioritize critical systems and assets based on their impact on the organization's mission and the potential risks involved. This includes identifying systems that handle sensitive data, such as customer information, financial records, and intellectual property. By understanding the criticality of these assets, IT professionals can allocate appropriate resources and implement enhanced security measures to protect them.

Additionally, IT professionals should consider the interconnectedness of their IT assets and systems. Many modern IT infrastructures rely on complex networks, cloud services, and third-party integrations. Understanding how these components interact and the potential risks they pose is crucial for maintaining a secure environment. By identifying dependencies and potential points of failure, IT professionals can implement preventative measures and develop effective incident response plans.

In the context of small businesses, implementing NIST SP 800-53 guidelines can seem daunting. However, this section aims to simplify the process by providing practical steps and recommendations tailored to small business environments. It will guide IT professionals through the process of mapping NIST controls to their identified assets and systems, ensuring a comprehensive and compliant security framework.

By identifying key IT assets and systems, IT professionals can gain a holistic understanding of their organization's security landscape. This knowledge enables them to make informed decisions and allocate resources effectively to protect critical assets and systems. Moreover, by implementing NIST SP 800-53 guidelines, small businesses can achieve compliance, enhance their security posture, and build trust with customers and partners.

In conclusion, this section provides a roadmap for IT professionals working in small businesses to identify key IT assets and systems. By conducting a thorough inventory assessment, prioritizing critical systems, and understanding inter-dependencies, IT professionals can build a strong foundation for implementing NIST SP 800-53 guidelines. This proactive approach to security not only mitigates risks but also ensures compliance and fosters a culture of cybersecurity within the organization.

Conducting a Risk Assessment for Small Business IT Infrastructure

In today's digital age, small businesses are more reliant on technology than ever before. With the increasing threats of cyberattacks and data breaches, small business IT professionals must prioritize the security of their infrastructure. One effective way to identify potential vulnerabilities and mitigate risks is through conducting a comprehensive risk assessment.

A risk assessment is a systematic process that involves identifying, analyzing, and evaluating potential risks to an organization's IT infrastructure. By conducting a risk assessment, IT professionals can determine the likelihood and impact of various threats, and develop effective strategies to address them. In the context of NIST SP 800-53 implementation for small businesses, a risk assessment is an essential step towards achieving compliance and ensuring the confidentiality, integrity, and availability of sensitive information.

The first step in conducting a risk assessment is to identify the assets within the IT infrastructure. This includes hardware, software, data, and personnel. IT professionals should create an inventory of all assets and classify them based on their criticality and sensitivity. By understanding the value and importance of each asset, it becomes easier to prioritize security measures and allocate resources accordingly.

Once the assets are identified, the next step is to identify potential threats and vulnerabilities. This can be done through internal and external assessments, such as network scans, penetration testing, and vulnerability assessments. IT professionals should also consider the potential impact of these threats, including financial, reputational, and legal consequences.

After identifying the threats and vulnerabilities, IT professionals should assess the likelihood and impact of each risk. This can be done using qualitative or quantitative risk assessment methods. Qualitative methods involve ranking risks based on their severity, while quantitative methods assign numerical values to each risk based on the probability and impact.

Based on the risk assessment results, IT professionals can then develop a risk mitigation plan. This plan should include specific actions to reduce or eliminate identified risks, such as implementing security controls, training employees on best practices, and regularly monitoring and updating systems.

Conducting a risk assessment is not a one-time activity but an ongoing process. IT professionals should regularly review and update their risk assessments to adapt to changing threats and technologies. By regularly assessing and addressing risks, small businesses can ensure the security and resilience of their IT infrastructure and maintain compliance with

NIST SP 800-53 standards.

In conclusion, conducting a risk assessment is a critical step for small business IT professionals seeking to implement NIST SP 800-53 standards. By identifying potential vulnerabilities and developing effective risk mitigation strategies, IT professionals can protect their infrastructure and sensitive information from cyber threats. Regularly reviewing and updating risk assessments will help small businesses stay proactive and compliant in an ever-evolving digital landscape.

Determining the Scope of NIST SP 800-53 Compliance for Small Businesses

As an IT professional, understanding the scope of NIST SP 800-53 compliance is crucial when implementing it for small businesses. NIST SP 800-53 is a comprehensive set of security controls and guidelines established by the National Institute of Standards and Technology (NIST) to protect sensitive information and systems from cyber threats. While it is primarily designed for federal agencies, many small businesses are now adopting these standards to enhance their cybersecurity posture and protect their valuable assets.

Determining the scope of NIST SP 800-53 compliance for small businesses involves several key considerations. First and foremost, it is important to assess the business's size, complexity, and the nature of its operations. Small businesses often have limited resources, both in terms of budget and personnel, making it essential to prioritize the implementation of controls based on risk assessment.

One approach is to perform a thorough inventory of the business's information systems, including hardware, software, and data assets. This inventory will help identify the systems that need to comply with NIST SP 800-53 controls and will guide the allocation of resources accordingly. It is important to remember that not all systems may require the same level of compliance, and a risk-based approach will help determine the appropriate level of controls for each system.

Moreover, small businesses must consider their industry-specific requirements and regulations. Certain industries, such as healthcare or finance, have additional compliance obligations that must be incorporated into the scope of NIST SP 800-53 implementation. Adhering to these industry-specific requirements ensures that the business is compliant not only with NIST standards but also with any relevant regulations.

Additionally, small businesses must assess their third-party relationships. If the business relies on vendors, cloud service providers, or other external parties to handle sensitive data, it is essential to include them in the scope of NIST SP 800-53 compliance. This involves evaluating the security controls and practices of these third parties to ensure they align with the desired level of security.

Overall, determining the scope of NIST SP 800-53 compliance for small businesses requires a comprehensive understanding of the organization's size, operations, industry requirements, and third-party relationships. By conducting a thorough assessment and risk analysis, IT professionals can effectively prioritize their efforts, allocate resources efficiently, and enhance the cybersecurity posture of the organization. Implementing NIST SP 800-53 controls will not only protect sensitive information but also instill confidence in customers, partners, and stakeholders that the business takes cybersecurity seriously.

Chapter 4: Implementing NIST SP 800-53 Controls for Small Businesses

Selecting Appropriate Controls for Small Business IT Environments

In today's digital era, small businesses are increasingly reliant on technology to streamline their operations and stay competitive. However, along with the benefits of technology come potential risks, making it crucial for small businesses to implement appropriate controls to safeguard their IT environments. This section aims to guide IT professionals in selecting the most suitable controls for small business IT environments, specifically focusing on NIST SP 800-53 implementation.

NIST SP 800-53 provides a comprehensive set of security and privacy controls that are widely recognized and adopted by organizations of all sizes. However, for small businesses, it is essential to streamline the control selection process to ensure efficiency and cost-effectiveness. Here are some key considerations to keep in mind when selecting controls for small business IT environments:

1. **Risk Assessment:** Begin by conducting a thorough risk assessment to

identify and prioritize the potential threats and vulnerabilities specific to your small business. This will help you determine which controls are most critical for mitigating these risks.

2. Tailoring Controls: NIST SP 800-53 offers a vast array of controls, but not all may be applicable or feasible for small businesses. Tailor the controls to fit your organization's size, resources, and unique requirements. Focus on controls that provide the maximum risk reduction for the investment made.

3. Cost-Effectiveness: Small businesses often operate with limited budgets. Consider the cost implications of implementing and maintaining each control. Look for cost-effective solutions that provide the necessary level of protection without burdening your financial resources.

4. Scalability: As small businesses grow and evolve, their IT environments will change. Select controls that can adapt and scale with your organization's needs, ensuring long-term sustainability and flexibility.

5. Compliance Requirements: Depending on your industry, small businesses may be subject to various compliance regulations. Ensure that the selected controls align with the applicable regulatory requirements to ensure compliance.

6. Training and Awareness: Controls are only effective if employees are aware of and trained in their implementation. Invest in training programs to ensure that your staff understands the importance of controls and their role in maintaining a secure IT environment.

By carefully considering these factors, small business IT professionals can confidently select controls that align with their organization's needs, resources, and compliance obligations. Remember, the goal is not to implement every control in NIST SP 800-53, but rather to create a robust and tailored control framework that effectively mitigates the risks specific to your small business IT environment.

Implementing Security Controls for System and Information Integrity

In today's digital age, ensuring the security and integrity of systems and information is of utmost importance for businesses, regardless of their size. Small businesses often face unique challenges when it comes to implementing security controls, particularly those outlined in the NIST SP 800-53 framework. However, with the right roadmap and guidance, small business IT professionals can effectively navigate the complex landscape of security compliance.

This section aims to provide IT professionals with a comprehensive understanding of the process and best practices for implementing security controls for system and information integrity. By following these guidelines, small businesses can enhance their security posture and protect their critical assets from potential threats.

The first step in implementing security controls is to conduct a comprehensive risk assessment. This involves identifying potential vulnerabilities and threats that could compromise the integrity of systems and information. By understanding the risks, businesses can prioritize their security efforts and allocate resources accordingly.

Once the risks have been identified, IT professionals can proceed to select and implement appropriate security controls. The NIST SP 800-53 framework provides a comprehensive set of controls that cover various aspects of system and information integrity. These controls include access controls, audit and accountability measures, configuration management, and system integrity monitoring, among others.

To ensure successful implementation, IT professionals should follow a systematic approach. This includes documenting policies and procedures, training employees on security best practices, and regularly monitoring and assessing the effectiveness of implemented controls. Regular audits and assessments will help identify any gaps or weaknesses in the security infrastructure, allowing for timely remediation.

Moreover, small businesses can leverage the expertise of third-party vendors and security professionals to streamline the implementation process. Partnering with managed security service providers or consultants specializing in NIST SP 800-53 implementation can provide small businesses with the necessary guidance and support to meet compliance requirements.

By implementing robust security controls for system and information integrity, small businesses can minimize the risk of data breaches, unauthorized access, and other security incidents. This not only protects sensitive information but also safeguards the reputation and trust of their customers.

The purpose of this section is to provide a comprehensive roadmap for small business IT professionals looking to implement NIST SP 800-53 within their organizations. By adhering to this widely recognized framework, small businesses can enhance their security posture and ensure the confidentiality, integrity, and availability of their information assets.

Below is a comprehensive roadmap for IT professionals looking to implement NIST SP 800-53 within their organizations:

Phase 1: Pre-Assessment Preparation

1. Management Buy-In:
   - Gain support from executive leadership for the NIST SP 800-53 implementation.
   - Communicate the importance of cybersecurity and compliance.

2. Assemble a Project Team:
   - Form a dedicated team with representatives from IT, security, legal, and other relevant departments.

3. Identify Assets and Data:
   - Conduct an inventory of all IT assets and sensitive data.
   - Identify systems, applications, and information that require protection.

Phase 2: Risk Assessment and Categorization

4. Conduct a Risk Assessment:
   - Identify potential threats and vulnerabilities.
   - Evaluate the impact and likelihood of various risks.

5. Categorize Information Systems:
   - Categorize information systems based on the impact levels outlined in NIST SP 800-53.

6. Prioritize Risks:

   - Prioritize risks based on severity and potential impact.

   - Use the risk assessment to guide control implementation priorities.

Phase 3: Develop Policies and Procedures

7. Develop Security Policies:

   - Establish comprehensive security policies based on NIST SP 800-53 controls.

   - Ensure policies align with the organization's risk tolerance and regulatory requirements.

8. Create Procedures:

   - Develop detailed procedures for implementing each security control.

   - Clearly document steps for incident response, configuration management, access control, etc.

Phase 4: Implement Security Controls

9. Access Control (AC):

   - Implement access control mechanisms, including unique user accounts and multi-factor authentication.

10. Configuration Management (CM):

    - Establish baseline configurations and a change control process.

11. Audit and Accountability (AU):

    - Enable auditing on systems, define auditable events, and set up audit record storage.

12. Security Assessment and Authorization (CA):

- Develop a security authorization process and continuously monitor security controls.

13. Security Training and Awareness (AT):
   - Implement security awareness training for employees.

14. Incident Response (IR):
   - Develop and implement an incident response plan.
   - Conduct regular training and exercises.

Phase 5: Documentation and Training

15. Document Everything:
   - Maintain comprehensive documentation for policies, procedures, and implemented controls.

16. Training and Awareness:
   - Train employees on security policies and procedures.
   - Foster a culture of security awareness and responsibility.

Phase 6: Continuous Monitoring and Improvement

17. Continuous Monitoring (CM):
   - Implement continuous monitoring of security controls.
   - Regularly assess and update security measures.

18. Incident Response (IR):
   - Regularly test incident response capabilities.
   - Review and update incident response plans.

19. Security Assessment and Authorization (CA):

- Conduct regular security assessments and update authorizations.

Phase 7: Compliance Validation

20. Internal Audits:
    - Conduct internal audits to validate compliance with NIST SP 800-53.
    - Address any identified gaps and areas for improvement.

21. Third-Party Assessment:
    - Consider engaging third-party assessors for an independent evaluation.
    - Address findings and enhance security controls as needed.

Phase 8: Ongoing Review and Enhancement

22. Review and Update:
    - Regularly review and update security policies and procedures.
    - Stay informed about changes in technology, regulations, and threat landscapes.

23. Continuous Improvement:
    - Embrace a culture of continuous improvement.
    - Encourage feedback and lessons learned to enhance the effectiveness of security controls.

24. Stay Informed:
    - Monitor NIST updates and revisions to SP 800-53.
    - Adjust security measures accordingly to align with the latest best practices.

By following the guidance provided in this section, small business

IT professionals can lay a solid foundation for information security within their organizations. Implementing NIST SP 800-53 will not only enhance the overall security posture but also instill confidence in customers, partners, and stakeholders, ultimately leading to business growth and success in today's digital economy.

In conclusion, this section serves as a roadmap for small business IT professionals looking to implement security controls for system and information integrity. By following the guidelines outlined in the NIST SP 800-53 framework and adopting best practices, small businesses can enhance their security posture, comply with industry regulations, and protect their critical assets.

Ensuring Access Control and User Authentication in Small Business IT Systems

In today's digital landscape, small businesses are increasingly becoming targets for cyber attacks. As a small business IT professional, it is crucial to prioritize access control and user authentication to safeguard your organization's sensitive information. This section will guide you through the essential steps to ensure robust access control and user authentication in your small business IT systems, specifically focusing on NIST SP 800-53 implementation.

Access control is the foundation of any secure IT system. It allows you to limit access to critical data and resources, ensuring that only authorized individuals can gain entry. To establish effective access control, start by conducting a thorough inventory of your organization's assets, identifying the most valuable resources that need protection.

Utilize NIST SP 800-53 guidelines to create access control policies and procedures tailored to your small business environment.

User authentication is another vital component of securing your IT systems. It verifies the identity of individuals attempting to access your network, applications, or data. Implement strong password policies, enforcing the use of complex passwords and regular password changes. Explore multi-factor authentication (MFA) options, such as biometrics or hardware tokens, to enhance user authentication security.

Implementing role-based access control (RBAC) is highly recommended for small businesses. RBAC assigns access privileges based on job roles, ensuring that employees have only the permissions necessary to perform their duties. Regularly review and update user access privileges to prevent unauthorized access and minimize potential risks.

Small businesses often struggle with limited resources and a lack of dedicated IT staff. However, automating access control and user authentication processes can help mitigate these challenges. Implement centralized identity and access management (IAM) solutions to stream-line user provisioning, deprovisioning, and access request processes. Leverage user activity monitoring tools to detect and respond to any suspicious activities promptly.

Regular training and awareness programs are essential to ensure that employees understand the importance of access control and user authen-tication. Educate your staff about phishing attacks, social engineering tactics, and best practices for creating strong passwords. Reinforce the significance of reporting any suspicious activities or potential security incidents.

By prioritizing access control and user authentication in your small business IT systems, you are taking significant steps towards securing your organization's digital assets. Following NIST SP 800-53 guidelines and implementing robust access control measures will help protect your sensitive data, maintain compliance, and instill confidence in customers and stakeholders. Remember, cybersecurity is an ongoing process, and regular assessments and updates are crucial to stay ahead of evolving threats.

Chapter 5: Developing Security Policies and Procedures

Creating an Information Security Policy for Small Business IT Professionals

In today's digital age, information security has become a critical concern for businesses of all sizes. Small businesses, in particular, face unique challenges when it comes to implementing robust security measures due to limited resources and expertise. However, with the right guidance and understanding of industry best practices, small business IT professionals can create an effective information security policy that aligns with the National Institute of Standards and Technology (NIST) Special Publication (SP) 800-53.

This roadmap provides small business IT professionals with a step-by-step guide to developing an effective Information Security Policy:

1. Define Scope and Objectives:
   - Identify Information Assets: Enumerate all digital assets and sensitive information.
   - Establish Objectives: Clearly define the goals and objectives of the

Information Security Policy.

2. Conduct a Risk Assessment:

- Identify Risks: Assess potential risks to information assets.
- Evaluate Impact and Likelihood: Determine the impact and likelihood of identified risks.

3. Compliance Requirements:

- Research Applicable Regulations: Identify and understand relevant industry regulations and compliance requirements.
- Incorporate Legal Standards: Ensure the Information Security Policy aligns with applicable laws and regulations.

4. Involve Stakeholders:

- Collaborate with Management: Engage with key stakeholders, including management and IT teams.
- Seek Input from Employees: Gather insights and feedback from employees to ensure comprehensive coverage.

5. Develop Policy Components:

- Access Control: Define access control policies for systems and data.
- Data Protection: Establish guidelines for data classification, encryption, and storage.
- Incident Response: Develop procedures for reporting and responding to security incidents.
- Employee Training: Outline ongoing training programs for employees on security best practices.

6. Document Policies and Procedures:

- Create Clear Documentation: Develop detailed and understandable policies and procedures.

- Version Control: Implement a version control system for policy documents.

7. Communication and Awareness:

- Internal Communication: Communicate the policy changes and expectations to all employees.

- Training Sessions: Conduct training sessions to ensure awareness and understanding.

8. Implement Technical Controls:

- Access Management: Implement access controls and user authentication mechanisms.

- Firewalls and Intrusion Detection Systems: Deploy technical measures to protect against unauthorized access and monitor network traffic.

9. Regular Audits and Assessments:

- Internal Audits: Conduct regular internal audits to assess policy adherence.

- External Assessments: Engage external auditors periodically for an independent evaluation.

10. Incident Response Plan:

- Develop Incident Response Procedures: Outline step-by-step procedures for handling security incidents.

- Regular Drills: Conduct regular drills to test the effectiveness of the incident response plan.

11. Monitoring and Continuous Improvement:

- Implement Monitoring Systems: Deploy continuous monitoring tools to detect and respond to security events.

- Feedback Loop: Establish a feedback loop for continuous improvement based on incidents and audits.

12. Review and Update:

- Regular Reviews: Schedule regular reviews of the Information Security Policy.

- Update as Needed: Update the policy in response to changes in technology, regulations, or business processes.

13. Employee Acknowledgment:

- Acknowledge Receipt: Require all employees to acknowledge receipt of and adherence to the Information Security Policy.

- Regular Training Refreshers: Provide periodic refresher training to employees.

14. Legal Consultation:

- Seek Legal Advice: Consult legal professionals to ensure compliance with local and industry-specific laws.

- Privacy Considerations: Address privacy concerns and incorporate relevant legal guidance.

15. Backup and Recovery:

- Establish Backup Procedures: Develop and implement backup procedures for critical data.

- Recovery Plans: Develop plans for data recovery in case of incidents.

16. Vendor Management:

- Include Third-Party Assessments: If applicable, include policies for assessing and managing security risks associated with third-party vendors.

17. Documentation Repository:

- Centralized Repository: Maintain a centralized repository for all documentation related to the Information Security Policy.

- Access Controls: Implement access controls to protect sensitive policy documents.

18. Create an Incident Reporting Mechanism:

- Clear Reporting Channels: Establish clear channels for reporting security incidents.

- Anonymity Considerations: Consider providing anonymous reporting options.

19. Regular Training and Awareness Programs:

- Continuous Education: Conduct ongoing training sessions to keep employees informed about evolving threats.

- Periodic Assessments: Administer periodic assessments to ensure employee understanding.

20. Seek Continuous Feedback:

- Employee Feedback: Encourage employees to provide feedback on the effectiveness of security controls.

- Adapt Based on Feedback: Use feedback to make continuous improvements to the Information Security Policy.

By following this roadmap, small business IT professionals can create a comprehensive Information Security Policy that not only complies with regulations but also fosters a culture of security awareness and resilience within the organization.

Establishing Incident Response and Business Continuity Plans

In today's digital landscape, where cyber threats are increasing in both sophistication and frequency, small businesses must have robust incident response and business continuity plans in place. As an IT professional, it is your responsibility to ensure the security and resilience of your organization's systems and data. This section will guide you through the process of establishing these plans, specifically tailored to the needs of small businesses implementing NIST SP 800-53.

An incident response plan is a proactive approach to handling and mitigating security incidents in a timely and effective manner. It outlines the roles, responsibilities, and procedures that should be followed when an incident occurs. The first step in establishing an incident response plan is to conduct a thorough risk assessment, identifying potential vulnerabilities and threats specific to your organization. This will help you prioritize your efforts and allocate resources accordingly.

Next, you need to define the incident response team, consisting of key personnel from various departments, such as IT, legal, and management. Each member should be assigned specific roles and responsibilities, ensuring a coordinated and efficient response. The plan should also include contact information for external resources, such as law enforcement agencies and incident response consultants, who can provide additional expertise and support when needed.

Once the incident response team is in place, it is essential to establish a communication plan. This includes both internal and external communication channels, ensuring that stakeholders are informed promptly and accurately. It is also crucial to define the escalation process, determining when and how to escalate incidents based on their severity and impact.

In addition to incident response, small businesses must also develop a business continuity plan. This plan outlines the strategies and procedures that will enable the organization to continue operating during and after a disruptive event, such as a cyber-attack or natural disaster. It should include measures to protect critical data, maintain essential functions, and restore normal operations as quickly as possible.

To ensure the effectiveness of both plans, regular testing and updating are necessary. Conducting mock incident scenarios and tabletop exercises will help identify any weaknesses or gaps in your response capabilities. It is also essential to stay up to date with the latest threats and vulnerabilities, adjusting your plans accordingly.

By establishing comprehensive incident response and business continuity plans, small businesses can effectively mitigate the impact of security incidents and ensure the continuity of their operations. Implementing NIST SP 800-53 guidelines provides a solid framework for developing these plans, enabling IT professionals to navigate the complex landscape of cybersecurity and compliance.

Documenting Security Procedures and Guidelines for Small Business IT Operations

In today's digital landscape, small businesses face an ever-increasing number of cyber threats. As an IT professional, it is crucial to ensure that your organization has robust security procedures and guidelines in place to protect sensitive data and mitigate potential risks. This section aims to provide you with a comprehensive understanding of documenting security procedures and guidelines for small business IT operations, specifically focusing on NIST SP 800-53 implementation.

The first step in documenting security procedures and guidelines is conducting a comprehensive risk assessment. This process involves identifying potential threats, vulnerabilities, and impacts to your IT operations. By understanding your organization's risk profile, you can prioritize security measures and allocate resources effectively.

Next, you need to develop a set of security policies and procedures tailored to your small business. These policies should address various aspects, including access control, incident response, data classification, and employee awareness training. They should be concise, easy to understand, and align with the objectives outlined in NIST SP 800-53.

To ensure consistent implementation, it is important to establish clear roles and responsibilities within your organization. Designate individuals who will be responsible for enforcing security policies and procedures, as well as conducting regular audits to assess compliance. Document these roles and responsibilities to provide clarity and accountability.

Additionally, documenting security procedures and guidelines should include the creation of incident response plans. These plans outline the steps to be taken in the event of a security breach or incident. They should detail the incident reporting process, communication channels, and containment measures to minimize the impact of the incident.

Regularly reviewing and updating your security procedures and guidelines is crucial to stay ahead of evolving threats. As new vulnerabilities emerge or regulations change, it is essential to adapt your security program accordingly. Documenting these updates and ensuring their dissemination throughout the organization is vital to maintaining a strong security posture.

In conclusion, documenting security procedures and guidelines for small business IT operations is a critical component of ensuring the protection of sensitive data. By following the guidelines outlined in NIST SP 800-53, you can establish a robust security program that mitigates risks and safeguards your organization. Regularly reviewing and updating these procedures will enable you to stay ahead of emerging threats and maintain a strong security posture in today's ever-evolving digital landscape.

Chapter 6: Security Awareness and Training for Small Business IT Professionals

Importance of Security Awareness and Training Programs for Small Business IT Staff

In today's interconnected world, small businesses are increasingly becoming targets of cyber threats. Hackers are constantly on the lookout for vulnerabilities in IT systems, and small businesses often lack the resources and expertise to defend against such attacks. This is where security awareness and training programs play a crucial role in safeguarding the IT infrastructure of small businesses.

The NIST SP 800-53 Implementation for Small Businesses provides a comprehensive roadmap for ensuring compliance with the necessary security controls. However, compliance alone is not enough to protect a company's sensitive data and critical systems. Small business IT staff needs to understand the importance of security awareness and be trained to identify and respond to potential threats effectively.

One of the key benefits of security awareness and training programs is the ability to create a security-conscious culture within the organization.

By educating IT staff about the latest threats and best practices, small businesses can foster a sense of responsibility and vigilance among their employees. This, in turn, reduces the likelihood of human errors or negligence that could lead to security breaches.

Furthermore, security awareness training equips IT staff with the knowledge and skills necessary to identify and mitigate various types of cyber threats. They learn how to recognize suspicious emails, avoid clicking on malicious links, and detect signs of a potential data breach. By empowering employees with this knowledge, small businesses can significantly reduce the risk of falling victim to cyberattacks.

Another important aspect of security awareness and training programs is their role in ensuring compliance with regulatory requirements. Small businesses are often subject to industry-specific regulations that mandate certain security controls. By providing training on these specific requirements, IT professionals can ensure that the business remains compliant and avoids potential penalties or legal consequences.

Lastly, security awareness and training programs also contribute to the overall resilience of small businesses. In the event of a security incident, a well-trained IT staff can respond promptly and effectively, minimizing the damage and downtime. This ability to quickly recover from an attack is crucial for the survival and reputation of a small business.

In conclusion, security awareness and training programs are essential for small businesses to protect their IT infrastructure and sensitive data. By fostering a security-conscious culture, equipping IT staff with the necessary knowledge and skills, ensuring compliance, and enhancing overall resilience, small businesses can effectively defend against cyber threats and secure their future. Implementing the recommendations outlined in the NIST SP 800-53 Implementation for Small Businesses will serve as a valuable guide in this journey towards a secure and resilient IT environment.

Designing and Implementing Security Training Initiatives

In today's digital landscape, cybersecurity threats continue to evolve and pose significant risks to businesses of all sizes. Small businesses, in particular, are increasingly becoming targets of cyber attacks due to their perceived vulnerability. To mitigate these risks, small businesses must prioritize security training initiatives that align with the NIST SP 800-53 guidelines. This section will delve into the key considerations and best practices for designing and implementing effective security training initiatives tailored to the needs of small businesses.

Understanding the NIST SP 800-53 framework is the first step towards compliance for small businesses. This comprehensive set of security controls provides a roadmap for organizations to safeguard their information systems against potential threats. However, compliance alone is not enough; it is essential to cultivate a security-conscious culture within the organization. This is where security training initiatives play a pivotal role.

The design of security training initiatives should be tailored to address the specific needs and challenges faced by small businesses. One-size-fits-all approaches are often ineffective and fail to resonate with employees. To ensure maximum impact, training programs should be interactive, engaging, and practical. This can include simulations, real-life scenarios, and hands-on exercises that allow employees to apply their knowledge in a safe environment.

Furthermore, it is crucial to establish clear learning objectives and measurable outcomes for each training session. This helps in assessing the effectiveness of the program and identifying areas that require improvement. Regular assessments and evaluations should be conducted to ensure that employees are retaining the knowledge and skills acquired during the training.

To foster a culture of continuous learning, small businesses should consider implementing ongoing security awareness programs. This includes providing updates on emerging threats, industry best practices, and new technologies that can enhance the security posture of the organization. Additionally, establishing a reporting mechanism for employees to report suspicious activities or potential breaches can contribute to early detection and response.

Small businesses often face resource constraints when it comes to security training initiatives. However, leveraging existing resources and partnering with external experts can help overcome these challenges. Collaborating with industry associations, government agencies, or security vendors can provide access to training materials, tools, and expertise that may otherwise be out of reach.

In conclusion, designing and implementing security training initiatives are critical for small businesses aiming to achieve compliance with the NIST SP 800-53 guidelines. By adopting a tailored approach, establishing clear objectives, fostering a culture of continuous learning, and leveraging available resources, small businesses can enhance their security posture and protect themselves against evolving cyber threats.

Measuring the Effectiveness of Security Awareness Programs for Small Businesses

In today's digital landscape, small businesses face an ever-increasing number of cybersecurity threats. To protect their sensitive data and maintain trust with customers, small businesses must implement effective security awareness programs. However, measuring the effectiveness of these programs can be a daunting task. This section aims to provide IT professionals in the niche of NIST SP 800-53 implementation for small businesses with valuable insights on how to measure the effectiveness of security awareness programs.

When it comes to measuring effectiveness, it is essential to establish clear goals and objectives for the security awareness program. These goals should be aligned with the organization's overall security strategy and should encompass specific outcomes, such as reducing the number of security incidents or improving employee knowledge and behavior. By setting measurable goals, IT professionals can track the progress of their security awareness program.

One common method for measuring effectiveness is through security awareness training assessments. These assessments can be conducted before and after the implementation of the program to gauge the improvement in employees' knowledge and awareness. By comparing the results, IT professionals can identify areas of strength and weakness and make necessary adjustments to the program.

Another crucial aspect of measuring effectiveness is monitoring the organization's security incident rates and patterns. By analyzing the frequency and severity of security incidents, IT professionals can determine if the security awareness program has had a positive impact on reducing incidents. Additionally, monitoring employee compliance with security policies and procedures can provide valuable insights into the effectiveness of the program.

Feedback and surveys can also be valuable tools for measuring effectiveness. By collecting feedback from employees regarding the security awareness program, IT professionals can gain insights into its perceived effectiveness and make improvements accordingly. Surveys can be conducted to gauge employees' understanding of security practices and to identify areas where additional training or resources may be required.

Furthermore, IT professionals can leverage metrics such as phishing simulation results, incident response times, and employee reporting rates to measure the effectiveness of security awareness programs. These metrics can provide tangible evidence of the program's impact on reducing vulnerabilities and improving incident response capabilities.

In conclusion, measuring the effectiveness of security awareness programs for small businesses is crucial to ensure their success in mitigating cybersecurity risks. By setting clear goals, conducting assessments, monitoring incident rates, collecting feedback, and leveraging metrics, IT professionals can gain valuable insights into the program's impact and make informed decisions to enhance its effectiveness. A comprehensive measurement strategy will not only help small businesses stay compliant with NIST SP 800-53 but also strengthen their overall cybersecurity posture.

Chapter 7: Continuous Monitoring and Improvement

Implementing Ongoing Security Monitoring Practices for Small Business IT Infrastructure

As an IT professional working in the small business sector, understanding and implementing ongoing security monitoring practices is essential for safeguarding your organization's IT infrastructure. In today's ever-evolving threat landscape, small businesses are increasingly becoming targets of cyberattacks, making it crucial to stay vigilant and proactive in your security efforts. This section will guide you through the process of implementing ongoing security monitoring practices based on the NIST SP 800-53 framework, specifically tailored for small businesses.

1. Importance of Ongoing Security Monitoring:

Effective security monitoring enables you to detect and respond to potential threats or vulnerabilities in your IT infrastructure promptly. By implementing continuous monitoring practices, you can identify suspicious activities, unauthorized access attempts, or anomalous behavior that may indicate a breach. This section will help you understand the significance of ongoing security monitoring in safeguarding your small business's IT systems and data.

2. Key Elements of Ongoing Security Monitoring:

This section will delve into the fundamental components of ongoing security monitoring for small business IT infrastructure. It will cover topics such as log management, intrusion detection and prevention systems, network monitoring, vulnerability scanning, and incident response. By implementing these key elements, you can establish a robust security monitoring framework to protect your organization from potential threats.

Ongoing security monitoring is a crucial aspect of any robust cybersecurity program. It involves the continuous observation, analysis, and assessment of an organization's information systems to identify and respond to security incidents. The goal is to maintain a proactive stance against potential threats and ensure the confidentiality, integrity, and availability of sensitive data. Here are key elements of ongoing security monitoring:

Continuous Threat Detection:
 - Employ advanced threat detection tools and technologies to monitor network traffic, system logs, and user activities in real-time.
 - Use intrusion detection systems (IDS), intrusion prevention systems (IPS), and security information and event management (SIEM) solutions to identify and alert on potential security incidents.

Log Management:
 - Implement centralized log management to collect, store, and analyze logs from various systems and applications.

- Regularly review and analyze log data to detect anomalies, unauthorized access, and potential security incidents.

Vulnerability Management:
- Conduct regular vulnerability assessments to identify weaknesses in systems and applications.
- Prioritize and address vulnerabilities based on their severity and potential impact on the organization.

Incident Response Planning:
- Develop and maintain an incident response plan that outlines the steps to be taken in the event of a security incident.
- Regularly update and test the incident response plan to ensure its effectiveness.

User and Entity Behavior Analytics (UEBA):
- Implement UEBA tools to analyze and identify unusual patterns of behavior among users and entities.
- Detect and respond to insider threats or compromised accounts by monitoring deviations from normal user behavior.

Network Security Monitoring:
- Employ network security monitoring tools to analyze network traffic and detect unusual or suspicious activities.
- Monitor for signs of malware, unauthorized access, or data exfiltration.

Endpoint Security:
- Utilize endpoint detection and response (EDR) solutions to monitor activities on individual devices.
- Implement controls to prevent and detect malware and unauthorized

access on endpoints.

Threat Intelligence Integration:

- Integrate threat intelligence feeds to stay informed about the latest cybersecurity threats.

- Use threat intelligence to enhance monitoring capabilities and proactively defend against emerging threats.

Regular Security Audits and Assessments:

- Conduct periodic security audits and assessments to evaluate the effectiveness of security controls.

- Identify and address gaps or weaknesses in the security posture.

Security Awareness Training:

- Educate employees on security best practices and the importance of reporting suspicious activities.

- Encourage a culture of security awareness to enhance the human element of ongoing monitoring.

Continuous Security Review:

- Regularly review and update security policies and procedures to address emerging threats and compliance requirements.

- Adapt security measures based on lessons learned from security incidents and audits.

Automated Response Mechanisms:

- Implement automated response mechanisms to rapidly respond to common security incidents.

- Automate repetitive tasks to free up resources for more complex threat analysis.

Regular Reporting and Communication:

- Generate regular reports on security metrics and incidents for management and stakeholders.

- Establish clear communication channels to ensure all relevant parties are informed during and after security incidents.

Legal and Compliance Considerations:

- Ensure ongoing monitoring activities align with legal and compliance requirements specific to the organization's industry and jurisdiction.

- Regularly review and update monitoring processes to maintain compliance.

Documentation and Documentation:

- Maintain comprehensive documentation of ongoing monitoring processes, tools, and activities.

- Document incident response procedures, lessons learned, and improvements for future reference.

Ongoing security monitoring is a dynamic and evolving process that requires a combination of technology, processes, and human expertise. By integrating these key elements, organizations can significantly enhance their ability to detect, respond to, and mitigate cybersecurity threats promptly.

3. Implementing NIST SP 800-53 for Ongoing Security Monitoring:

NIST SP 800-53 provides a comprehensive set of security controls and guidelines widely recognized as the gold standard for federal agencies. This section will outline how small businesses can implement relevant controls from NIST SP 800-53 to strengthen their ongoing security monitoring practices. It will provide practical insights and step-by-step instructions on customizing these controls to suit the specific needs and constraints of small businesses.

4. Leveraging Automation and Threat Intelligence:

Automation and threat intelligence play a crucial role in effective security monitoring. This section will explore the use of automation tools and technologies that can streamline the monitoring process, enhance detection capabilities, and reduce human error. Additionally, it will discuss the importance of leveraging threat intelligence sources to stay updated on emerging threats and vulnerabilities.

5. Continuous Improvement and Adaptation:

The threat landscape is constantly evolving, making ongoing security monitoring an iterative process. This section will emphasize the importance of continuous improvement and adaptation to stay ahead of potential threats. It will provide guidance on establishing a feedback loop, conducting regular assessments, and adjusting security monitoring practices accordingly.

By implementing ongoing security monitoring practices based on the NIST SP 800-53 framework, small businesses can enhance their cybersecurity posture and effectively protect their IT infrastructure. This section serves as a roadmap for IT professionals working in small businesses, providing practical insights and actionable steps to implement a robust security monitoring program. Stay proactive, continuously monitor, and protect your organization from cyber threats.

Conducting Periodic Security Assessments and Audits

In today's digital landscape, where cyber threats are becoming increasingly sophisticated and prevalent, small businesses must prioritize the security of their IT infrastructure. To ensure the protection of sensitive information, comply with regulations, and maintain a strong cybersecurity posture, regular security assessments and audits are essential.

A security assessment is a comprehensive evaluation of an organization's IT systems, networks, and processes to identify vulnerabilities and weaknesses. It involves analyzing the effectiveness of existing security controls, identifying potential risks, and recommending improvements to enhance the overall security posture. By conducting periodic security assessments, small businesses can proactively identify and address vulnerabilities before they are exploited by malicious actors.

Audits, on the other hand, are formal examinations of an organization's security controls, policies, and procedures to ensure compliance with specific standards or regulations, such as NIST SP 800-53. These audits provide an independent and objective assessment of the organization's security practices. They help small businesses identify gaps in their security implementation and ensure alignment with the recommended security controls.

To successfully conduct periodic security assessments and audits, IT professionals need to follow a systematic approach. First and foremost, a well-defined scope and objective should be established for each assessment or audit. This ensures that the evaluation is focused and tailored to the specific needs of the organization.

The next step involves gathering relevant information about the IT infrastructure, including network architecture, hardware and software assets, user access controls, and data flow diagrams. This information will serve as the basis for identifying potential vulnerabilities and risks.

Once the necessary information is collected, IT professionals can perform vulnerability scans, penetration tests, and security control assessments to identify weaknesses and measure the effectiveness of existing security controls. These tests simulate real-world attacks and attempt to exploit vulnerabilities, providing valuable insights into the organization's security posture.

After identifying vulnerabilities, IT professionals should prioritize and remediate them based on their potential impact and likelihood of exploitation. This may involve implementing additional security controls, updating software and systems, or improving security awareness training for employees.

Regularly conducting security assessments and audits is not only crucial for small businesses to comply with regulations but also to stay one step ahead of cyber threats. By proactively identifying vulnerabilities and implementing necessary security measures, IT professionals can help small businesses mitigate risks and ensure the confidentiality, integrity, and availability of their critical assets.

In conclusion, periodic security assessments and audits are vital for small businesses implementing NIST SP 800-53. They provide insights into vulnerabilities and weaknesses within the IT infrastructure, allowing IT professionals to take proactive measures to enhance security. By following a systematic approach, organizations can identify and remediate vulnerabilities, ensuring compliance, and maintaining a strong cybersecurity posture.

Incorporating Lessons Learned and Best Practices for Continuous Improvement

As IT professionals navigating the world of NIST SP 800-53 implementation for small businesses, continuous improvement is essential for ensuring the long-term success and compliance of your organization. This section explores the art of incorporating lessons learned and best practices into your operations, enabling you to enhance your security posture and stay ahead in an ever-evolving landscape.

Lessons learned play a crucial role in the growth of any organization. By reflecting on past experiences and identifying areas for improvement, you can avoid repeating mistakes and enhance your overall security posture. It is important to establish a culture of learning and knowledge sharing within your IT team, encouraging open communication and collaboration. Regular meetings or post-incident reviews can provide valuable insights into the root causes of security incidents or vulnerabilities, allowing you to implement effective countermeasures and prevent future occurrences.

Furthermore, incorporating best practices into your operations can significantly streamline your NIST SP 800-53 compliance journey. Familiarizing yourself with established frameworks, such as the Center for Internet Security (CIS) Controls or the National Cybersecurity Center of Excellence (NCCoE) guidelines, can provide a solid foundation for your security strategy. These frameworks offer comprehensive roadmaps that align with NIST SP 800-53 requirements and are tailored to the unique needs of small businesses.

Implementing continuous monitoring tools and practices is another effective way to embrace best practices. By leveraging technologies that provide real-time visibility into your network and systems, you can proactively identify and address potential vulnerabilities or threats. Regularly scanning your infrastructure, conducting penetration tests, and analyzing logs can help you detect and mitigate security issues before they escalate.

Additionally, staying updated with the latest industry trends and emerging threats is crucial for continuous improvement. Networking with other IT professionals, attending conferences, and participating in industry forums can expose you to valuable insights and innovative practices. Engaging with cybersecurity communities, such as the NIST Cybersecurity Framework (CSF) or the Small Business Administration (SBA) cybersecurity resources, can provide access to expert advice and relevant case studies.

Incorporating lessons learned and best practices for continuous improvement is not a one-time task but an ongoing process. By fostering a culture of learning, leveraging established frameworks, implementing continuous monitoring practices, and staying informed about industry trends, you can position your small business for long-term success and compliance with NIST SP 800-53. Embrace the journey of improvement, and let it be the driving force behind your organization's cybersecurity efforts.

Chapter 8: NIST SP 800-53 Compliance Reporting for Small Businesses

Understanding Compliance Reporting Requirements for Small Business IT Professionals

Compliance reporting is a critical aspect of ensuring the security and integrity of small business IT systems. As an IT professional, it is essential to comprehend the compliance reporting requirements outlined in NIST SP 800-53 to effectively implement them for small businesses. This section will provide you with a comprehensive understanding of compliance reporting and its significance in the context of small business IT.

Compliance reporting refers to the process of documenting and reporting on an organization's adherence to specific security controls and standards. For small businesses, compliance reporting plays a significant role in demonstrating their commitment to safeguarding sensitive information and meeting industry regulations. It provides a clear picture of the organization's security posture, aids in identifying vulnerabilities, and helps in making informed decisions for risk management.

NIST SP 800-53 serves as a comprehensive guide for small businesses to implement adequate security controls. However, understanding the reporting requirements under NIST SP 800-53 can be daunting. This section aims to break down these requirements into manageable steps, making it easier for IT professionals to navigate the compliance reporting process.

The first step in compliance reporting is understanding the scope of your organization's IT systems. This involves identifying the assets, systems, and information that fall under the purview of compliance reporting. Once the scope is defined, you can proceed with mapping the security controls outlined in NIST SP 800-53 to your organization's IT environment.

Next, you need to establish a reporting framework that aligns with the requirements of NIST SP 800-53. This framework should outline the frequency, format, and content of your compliance reports. It is crucial to ensure that your reports capture the necessary information, such as control implementation status, vulnerabilities, and any remediation actions taken.

Lastly, we will discuss best practices for compliance reporting, including maintaining accurate and up-to-date documentation, conducting regular audits, and engaging in continuous monitoring. These practices will help small businesses stay ahead of compliance requirements and address any gaps or vulnerabilities promptly.

By mastering compliance reporting requirements outlined in NIST SP 800-53, IT professionals can effectively guide small businesses toward achieving and maintaining a secure IT environment. This section will equip you with the knowledge and tools needed to streamline compliance reporting processes, demonstrate adherence to security controls, and ultimately safeguard sensitive information for small businesses.

Here are best practices for compliance reporting, including maintaining accurate and up-to-date documentation, conducting regular audits, and engaging in continuous monitoring.

Establish Clear Documentation Processes:

- Document All Policies and Procedures: Clearly document security policies, procedures, and controls in a centralized repository.

- Version Control: Implement version control mechanisms to track changes and ensure that documentation reflects the latest updates.

Conduct Regular Audits:

- Scheduled Audits: Conduct regular internal audits to assess compliance with established policies and procedures.

- Third-Party Audits: Engage external auditors periodically to provide an independent evaluation of compliance efforts.

Continuous Monitoring:

- Implement Security Information and Event Management (SIEM) Systems: Utilize SIEM tools for continuous monitoring of security events and incidents.

- Automate Monitoring Processes: Implement automated monitoring processes to detect deviations from established security baselines.

Automated Compliance Management Tools:

- Utilize Compliance Management Software: Invest in tools that automate compliance management tasks, streamline reporting, and facilitate evidence collection.

- Integration with IT Systems: Ensure that compliance tools integrate seamlessly with existing IT systems to gather real-time data.

Centralized Documentation Repository:

- Single Source of Truth: Maintain a centralized repository for all compliance-related documentation.

- Access Control: Implement access controls to ensure that only authorized personnel can modify or access sensitive compliance documentation.

Regular Training and Awareness Programs:

- Employee Education: Conduct regular training sessions to educate employees on compliance requirements and the importance of adherence.

- Awareness Campaigns: Promote a culture of compliance through awareness campaigns to keep employees informed about evolving threats and regulations.

Incident Response Planning:

- Include Compliance in Incident Response Plans: Integrate compliance considerations into incident response plans to ensure a coordinated response to security events.

- Documentation of Incident Responses: Document responses to incidents, including lessons learned and improvements for future prevention.

Continuous Improvement:

- Feedback Loops: Establish mechanisms for collecting feedback from audits, incidents, and monitoring activities.

- Iterative Improvement: Use feedback to continuously improve compliance processes, documentation, and controls.

Risk Assessment Integration:

- Integrate Compliance with Risk Assessments: Align compliance efforts with ongoing risk assessments to prioritize actions based on the organization's risk profile.

- Risk-Informed Decision Making: Make compliance decisions informed by risk assessments and threat intelligence.

Regular Reporting:

- Scheduled Reporting Cycles: Establish a regular reporting cycle for compliance reports, making it part of routine business operations.

- Customize Reports: Tailor reports to address specific stakeholder needs, whether for executive leadership, regulatory bodies, or internal teams.

Engage with Regulatory Bodies:

- Proactive Communication: Maintain open communication with relevant regulatory bodies.

- Seek Guidance: Seek guidance when uncertainties arise regarding compliance interpretations.

Cross-Functional Collaboration:

- Collaboration Between Departments: Foster collaboration between IT, security, legal, and other relevant departments to ensure a holistic approach to compliance.

- Regular Meetings: Conduct regular cross-functional meetings to discuss compliance challenges, progress, and upcoming requirements.

Documentation of Exception Handling:

- Exception Handling Process: Define a process for handling exceptions to compliance requirements.

- Document Rationale: Clearly document the rationale behind exceptions, including risk assessments and mitigation strategies.

External Benchmarking:

- Compare Against Industry Standards: Regularly benchmark compliance efforts against industry standards and best practices.

- Stay Informed: Stay informed about emerging threats and regulatory changes that might impact compliance requirements.

Data Integrity Measures:

- Data Validation Processes: Implement data validation processes to ensure the accuracy and integrity of compliance-related data.

- Regular Data Audits: Conduct regular audits of compliance-related data to identify and rectify discrepancies.

Legal and Ethical Considerations:

- Ethical Behavior Guidelines: Establish guidelines for ethical behavior related to compliance.

- Legal Consultation: Seek legal advice when navigating complex compliance issues to ensure proper adherence to legal requirements.

Regular Review of Controls Effectiveness:

- Effectiveness Metrics: Define and track metrics to measure the effectiveness of implemented controls.

- Adjust Controls as Needed: Regularly review control effectiveness and adjust them based on lessons learned from incidents and audits.

Compliance reporting is not a one-time activity but rather a continuous process that requires dedication and collaboration across the organization. By following these best practices, organizations can enhance their ability to demonstrate and maintain compliance, ultimately strengthening their overall cybersecurity posture.

Creating and Submitting Compliance Reports to Relevant Authorities

As IT professionals working in small businesses, it is crucial to understand the importance of compliance with the National Institute of Standards and Technology (NIST) Special Publication (SP) 800-53 guidelines. Compliance not only helps protect sensitive data but also ensures that your organization meets the requirements set by regulatory authorities.

Once you have implemented the necessary controls and measures to achieve compliance, the next step is to create and submit compliance reports to the relevant authorities. This section will guide you through this process, providing you with a roadmap to successfully navigate the complexities of compliance reporting.

First and foremost, it is essential to understand the specific requirements of the regulatory authorities that govern your industry. Familiarize yourself with the reporting standards and formats they expect from organizations like yours. This knowledge will help you tailor your compliance reports to meet their expectations accurately.

Next, you should establish a robust reporting framework within your organization. This framework should outline the reporting process, including the frequency of reporting, the responsible individuals or teams, and the tools or software used to generate reports. Having a well-defined framework in place will streamline the reporting process and ensure consistency.

The compliance reports you submit should provide a comprehensive overview of your organization's adherence to the NIST SP 800-53 guidelines. Include information on the controls implemented, any vulnerabilities identified, and the remediation measures taken to address those vulnerabilities. It is also essential to highlight any incidents or breaches that have occurred, along with the steps taken to mitigate their impact.

To make your compliance reports more effective, consider using visual aids such as graphs and charts to present data in a concise and understandable format. This will help the relevant authorities quickly assess your organization's compliance status and identify any areas that require further attention.

Finally, ensure that your compliance reports are submitted within the specified timelines. Late submissions can result in penalties and may negatively impact your organization's reputation. Establish a schedule for generating and submitting reports and assign responsibility to appropriate individuals to ensure timely delivery.

In conclusion, creating and submitting compliance reports to relevant authorities is a critical aspect of NIST SP 800-53 implementation for small businesses. By understanding the reporting requirements, establishing a robust reporting framework, and providing comprehensive and visually appealing reports, you can demonstrate your organization's commitment to compliance and protect sensitive data effectively.

Responding to Compliance Audit Findings and Corrective Actions

In today's digital landscape, compliance with industry standards and regulations is vital for businesses to ensure the security and integrity of their IT systems. Small businesses, in particular, face unique challenges in implementing and maintaining compliance with the National Institute of Standards and Technology (NIST) Special Publication (SP) 800-53.

This section aims to guide IT professionals in small businesses on how to effectively respond to compliance audit findings and implement corrective actions. It is essential to understand that compliance audits are conducted to assess the organization's adherence to the NIST SP 800-53 controls and identify any gaps or vulnerabilities. The audit findings serve as a roadmap for implementing appropriate corrective actions.

First and foremost, it is crucial to promptly acknowledge and address the audit findings. Ignoring or delaying the response can lead to severe consequences, including legal penalties, reputational damage, and loss of customer trust. IT professionals should establish a clear process for receiving, documenting, and prioritizing audit findings.

Once the findings are identified, IT professionals must conduct a thorough analysis to understand the root causes and implications. This analysis should involve collaboration with various stakeholders, including compliance officers, cybersecurity experts, and business leaders. By gaining a comprehensive understanding of the findings, the IT team can develop an effective action plan.

The next step is to prioritize the corrective actions based on their potential impact and feasibility. IT professionals need to assess the resources, time, and budget required for each action and prioritize them accordingly. It is essential to involve business leaders in this process to ensure alignment with organizational goals and objectives.

Implementing the corrective actions should be done with utmost care and attention to detail. IT professionals should establish a well-defined project management framework for tracking progress, assigning responsibilities, and monitoring timelines. Regular communication and collaboration with all stakeholders are vital to ensure smooth implementation.

After implementing the corrective actions, it is crucial to conduct a thorough review and validation of the changes made. This validation process should include re-auditing the controls to ensure their effectiveness and compliance with NIST SP 800-53 requirements. IT professionals should document the validation process to demonstrate their commitment to continuous improvement and compliance.

In conclusion, responding to compliance audit findings and implementing corrective actions is a critical process for small businesses aiming to achieve and maintain compliance with NIST SP 800-53. By promptly acknowledging and addressing the findings, conducting a thorough analysis, prioritizing the corrective actions, and implementing them effectively, IT professionals can ensure a secure and compliant IT infrastructure.

Chapter 9: NIST SP 800-53 Compliance Challenges and Solutions for Small Businesses

Common Challenges Faced by Small Business IT Professionals during NIST SP 800-53 Compliance

Implementing NIST SP 800-53 compliance standards can be a daunting task for any organization, but it poses unique challenges for small businesses. Small business IT professionals face a wide range of obstacles when it comes to achieving and maintaining NIST SP 800-53 compliance. In this section, we will explore some of the most common challenges faced by small business IT professionals during NIST SP 800-53 compliance and provide strategies to overcome them.

One of the major challenges faced by small business IT professionals is limited resources. Small businesses often operate with constrained budgets and limited staff, making it difficult to allocate resources for compliance efforts. This challenge can be addressed by adopting a risk-based approach to compliance, where IT professionals prioritize the most critical security controls and allocate resources accordingly. By focusing on the most significant risks, small businesses can optimize their compliance efforts and make the most out of their limited resources.

Another challenge faced by small business IT professionals is the lack of specialized expertise. NIST SP 800-53 compliance requires a deep understanding of security controls, risk assessments, and mitigation strategies. However, small businesses may not have dedicated security teams or personnel with the necessary expertise. To overcome this challenge, small business IT professionals can consider partnering with external consultants or leveraging online resources and training materials specifically tailored for small businesses.

Integration with existing systems and processes is another common challenge faced by small business IT professionals. Implementing NIST SP 800-53 compliance may require significant changes to existing IT systems and processes, which can be disruptive and time-consuming. To address this challenge, IT professionals can conduct a thorough assessment of their current systems and processes, identify gaps, and develop a roadmap for incremental changes. By taking a phased approach to implementation, small businesses can minimize disruptions and ensure a smooth transition to compliance.

Lastly, maintaining ongoing compliance is a challenge faced by small business IT professionals. Compliance is not a one-time effort but an ongoing process that requires continuous monitoring, updates, and improvements. Small businesses may struggle to allocate resources for ongoing compliance efforts due to competing priorities. To overcome this challenge, IT professionals can leverage automation tools and technologies that streamline compliance monitoring and reporting processes. Additionally, regular training and awareness programs can help ensure that employees understand their roles and responsibilities in maintaining compliance.

In conclusion, small business IT professionals face unique challenges when it comes to NIST SP 800-53 compliance. Limited resources, lack of specialized expertise, integration with existing systems, and maintaining ongoing compliance are some of the common hurdles they must overcome. By adopting a risk-based approach, leveraging external expertise, taking a phased implementation approach, and utilizing automation tools, small business IT professionals can successfully navigate the path to NIST SP 800-53 compliance and ensure the security of their organizations.

Strategies and Solutions to Overcome Compliance Challenges

In the dynamic landscape of cybersecurity, compliance with industry standards and regulations is of utmost importance for all organizations, regardless of their size. However, for small businesses, the task of implementing and maintaining compliance, specifically with NIST SP 800-53, can pose unique challenges. To address these challenges, IT professionals need to adopt effective strategies and solutions that align with the specific needs and resources of small businesses.

One of the key strategies to overcome compliance challenges is to develop a comprehensive understanding of the NIST SP 800-53 framework. IT professionals should familiarize themselves with the control families, standards, and guidelines outlined in the framework. This knowledge will enable them to identify and prioritize the controls that are most relevant to their organization's operations and risk profile.

Next, IT professionals should focus on building a strong compliance culture within the organization. This can be achieved by fostering awareness and education among employees about the importance of compliance and the role they play in maintaining it. Regular training sessions and communication channels should be established to keep employees informed about compliance requirements and best practices.

To ensure compliance with NIST SP 800-53, IT professionals should leverage technology solutions designed for small businesses. These solutions can automate various compliance processes, such as security assessments, documentation, and monitoring. By streamlining these tasks, small businesses can reduce the burden on their IT teams and ensure consistent compliance across all areas of their operations.

Collaboration with external partners and service providers is another valuable solution for small businesses grappling with compliance challenges. IT professionals should seek out vendors and consultants who specialize in NIST SP 800-53 implementation for small businesses. These experts can provide guidance, support, and resources tailored to the unique needs of small organizations, helping them overcome compliance hurdles more effectively.

Lastly, IT professionals should establish a robust incident response and recovery plan to mitigate the impact of potential security breaches or non-compliance incidents. This plan should include clear protocols for detecting, reporting, and addressing incidents promptly. Regular testing and evaluation of the plan's effectiveness are crucial to ensure its readiness in real-world scenarios.

In conclusion, small businesses face specific compliance challenges when implementing NIST SP 800-53. However, with the right strategies and solutions in place, IT professionals can successfully navigate these challenges. By developing a strong compliance culture, leveraging technology solutions, collaborating with external partners, and establishing a robust incident response plan, small businesses can achieve and maintain compliance with NIST SP 800-53, safeguarding their operations and data against cyber threats.

Case Studies and Success Stories of Small Businesses Achieving NIST SP 800-53 Compliance

In today's digital landscape, small businesses are increasingly becoming the target of cyber threats. As technology advances, so do the risks associated with storing and managing sensitive data. To mitigate these risks, the National Institute of Standards and Technology (NIST) developed a comprehensive set of security controls and guidelines called NIST SP 800-53.

Implementing NIST SP 800-53 compliance may seem like a daunting task for small businesses with limited resources and IT expertise. However, numerous success stories and case studies have emerged, highlighting the achievements of small businesses in achieving NIST SP 800-53 compliance. These inspiring examples serve as a roadmap for other IT professionals looking to secure their organization's data and systems effectively.

One such success story is ABC Technologies, a small IT services provider. Recognizing the importance of data security and client trust, ABC Technologies embarked on a journey to achieve NIST SP 800-53 compliance. By leveraging the available resources and employing a systematic approach, they successfully implemented the necessary security controls within their organization. This not only enhanced their cybersecurity posture but also allowed them to gain a competitive advantage by showcasing their commitment to data protection.

Another noteworthy case study is XYZ Solutions, a small software development company. XYZ Solutions was entrusted with developing software for a government agency, which required adherence to NIST SP 800-53 compliance. Initially overwhelmed by the complexity of the security controls, XYZ Solutions sought guidance from NIST experts and engaged in extensive training programs. Through perseverance and dedication, they were able to meet all the compliance requirements and deliver a secure solution to the government agency. This accomplishment not only solidified their reputation as a reliable vendor but also opened doors to new business opportunities.

These case studies demonstrate that small businesses, regardless of their limitations, can achieve NIST SP 800-53 compliance with the right approach and commitment. By investing in training, leveraging available resources, and seeking expert guidance when needed, IT professionals can navigate the intricate landscape of NIST SP 800-53 implementation successfully.

Moreover, achieving NIST SP 800-53 compliance offers numerous benefits beyond data protection. It increases customer trust, fosters business partnerships, and positions small businesses as reliable and secure technology providers. By showcasing their compliance with industry standards, small businesses can gain a competitive edge and attract clients who prioritize data security.

In conclusion, the success stories and case studies of small businesses achieving NIST SP 800-53 compliance serve as a source of inspiration and guidance for IT professionals. By following in their footsteps and adopting a systematic and dedicated approach, small businesses can effectively protect their data, enhance their cybersecurity posture, and elevate their reputation in the market. NIST SP 800-53 compliance is not only achievable but also beneficial for small businesses operating in today's digital age.

Chapter 10: Future Trends and Recommendations for Small Business IT Professionals

Emerging Trends in NIST SP 800-53 Compliance for Small Businesses

As IT professionals in the ever-evolving landscape of technology, staying up-to-date with the latest trends and compliance frameworks is crucial. One such framework that has gained prominence in recent years is the National Institute of Standards and Technology (NIST) Special Publication (SP) 800-53. In this section, we will explore the emerging trends in NIST SP 800-53 compliance specifically tailored for small businesses.

NIST SP 800-53 provides a comprehensive set of security controls and guidelines for federal information systems. While initially designed for government agencies, it has increasingly become a benchmark for organizations across various industries. Small businesses, in particular, have recognized the importance of aligning their security practices with NIST SP 800-53 to enhance their cybersecurity posture and meet regulatory requirements.

One emerging trend in NIST SP 800-53 compliance for small businesses is the adoption of cloud-based solutions. With the increasing reliance on cloud computing, small businesses are leveraging cloud service providers that offer NIST-compliant environments. This allows them to offload some of the security responsibilities to the provider while ensuring their data and systems are protected according to NIST SP 800-53 standards.

Another trend is the integration of automation tools for continuous monitoring and compliance management. Small businesses often have limited resources, making manual compliance monitoring a daunting task. By implementing automated tools, these organizations can streamline their compliance efforts, identify vulnerabilities in real-time, and generate reports for auditing purposes. This trend not only saves time and effort but also ensures that small businesses can proactively address security risks.

Furthermore, NIST SP 800-53 compliance is increasingly being viewed as a competitive advantage for small businesses. Many organizations now recognize that demonstrating compliance with NIST standards can enhance their reputation, build trust with customers, and open doors to new opportunities. As a result, small businesses are investing in NIST SP 800-53 compliance to differentiate themselves in the market and gain a competitive edge.

In conclusion, NIST SP 800-53 compliance is becoming a vital component for small businesses in ensuring their cybersecurity resilience. By adopting cloud-based solutions, leveraging automation tools, and viewing compliance as a competitive advantage, small businesses can align their security practices with NIST SP 800-53 and enhance their overall cybersecurity posture. As IT professionals, staying abreast of these emerging trends and helping small businesses navigate the complexities of NIST SP 800-53 compliance will be key to their success in the ever-evolving digital landscape.

Recommendations for Small Business IT Professionals to Stay Ahead in Compliance Efforts

In today's fast-paced and interconnected digital world, small businesses face significant challenges in ensuring their IT systems are compliant with government regulations, particularly those outlined in NIST SP 800-53. Compliance is not only crucial for avoiding penalties and legal consequences but also for safeguarding sensitive data and maintaining the trust of customers and partners.

To help small business IT professionals navigate the complex landscape of compliance, we have compiled a set of recommendations to stay ahead in their compliance efforts.

1. **Develop a Comprehensive Understanding:** Start by thoroughly studying the NIST SP 800-53 guidelines and familiarizing yourself with the specific requirements applicable to your industry and organization. Gain an in-depth understanding of different control families, their objectives, and how they relate to your business processes.

2. **Conduct a Gap Analysis:** Perform a thorough assessment of your current IT infrastructure, policies, and procedures to identify any gaps in compliance. This analysis will help you prioritize and allocate resources

effectively.

3. Implement a Risk Management Framework: Establish a robust risk management framework that aligns with NIST SP 800-53. This framework should include risk identification, assessment, mitigation, and ongoing monitoring to ensure compliance and provide a proactive approach to security.

4. Create a Compliance Roadmap: Develop a detailed roadmap that outlines specific actions, timelines, and responsible parties to achieve compliance. Breaking down the process into manageable steps will make it easier to track progress and address any issues that arise.

5. Train and Educate Employees: Compliance efforts should involve the entire organization. Conduct regular training sessions to educate employees about their roles and responsibilities in maintaining compliance. Emphasize the importance of data security and the consequences of non-compliance.

6. Engage External Experts: Small businesses often lack the internal resources and expertise required for full compliance. Consider partnering with external consultants or managed service providers who specialize in NIST SP 800-53 implementation for small businesses. Their knowledge and experience can significantly streamline the compliance journey.

7. Stay Updated: Compliance requirements are dynamic and subject to change. Stay informed about the latest updates and revisions to NIST SP 800-53. Regularly review and update your compliance program to ensure ongoing alignment with the latest standards.

8. Regularly Audit and Assess: Conduct regular audits and assessments to evaluate the effectiveness of your compliance program. Identify areas for improvement and take prompt action to address any deficiencies or vulnerabilities.

By following these recommendations, small business IT professionals can stay ahead in their compliance efforts, minimize risks, and maintain a secure and trustworthy IT environment. Remember, compliance is an ongoing process, and staying proactive is key to successfully navigating the ever-evolving regulatory landscape.

Leveraging NIST SP 800-53 Compliance for Business Growth and Competitive Advantage

In today's rapidly evolving business landscape, information security and compliance have become essential for organizations of all sizes. Small businesses, in particular, face unique challenges when it comes to meeting regulatory requirements, as they often lack the resources and expertise available to larger enterprises. However, complying with industry standards such as NIST SP 800-53 can not only ensure data protection but also offer opportunities for growth and competitive advantage.

Implementing NIST SP 800-53 compliance can bring several benefits to small businesses. Firstly, it instills trust and confidence among customers, partners, and stakeholders. In an era where data breaches and cyberattacks are becoming increasingly common, demonstrating a commitment to safeguarding sensitive information can differentiate a small business from its competitors. A strong security posture can be a powerful selling point, attracting customers who prioritize data privacy and protection.

Moreover, NIST SP 800-53 compliance can also enhance operational efficiency and reduce risks. By implementing the recommended security controls, small businesses can identify vulnerabilities and implement preventive measures to mitigate cyber threats. This proactive approach not only protects the organization's assets but also minimizes downtime and potential financial losses associated with security incidents.

Additionally, NIST SP 800-53 compliance can open doors to new business opportunities. Many government agencies and large corporations require their vendors and partners to meet specific security standards. By aligning with NIST guidelines, small businesses can position themselves as reliable and trusted partners for these entities, expanding their market reach and unlocking potential contracts and collaborations.

To leverage NIST SP 800-53 compliance for business growth, small businesses must approach it strategically. This involves understanding the specific requirements and tailoring the implementation process to suit their unique needs and resources. Engaging IT professionals with experience in NIST SP 800-53 implementation for small businesses can be invaluable in this regard, as they can provide the necessary expertise and guidance to navigate the compliance journey effectively.

In conclusion, NIST SP 800-53 compliance is not merely a regulatory burden for small businesses; it is an opportunity for growth and competitive advantage. By embracing these standards, organizations can enhance their reputation, streamline operations, reduce risks, and access new business opportunities. Investing in NIST SP 800-53 compliance is an investment in the future success and sustainability of small businesses in today's interconnected world.

Appendix A: Glossary of Terms

In the world of information technology (IT) and cybersecurity, understanding the terminology is crucial for effective communication and successful implementation of standards and frameworks. This glossary of terms aims to provide IT professionals, specifically those working in small businesses, with a comprehensive reference to the key terms associated with NIST SP 800-53 implementation.

Access Control: The process of managing and restricting access to resources, systems, or data, ensuring only authorized individuals can obtain access while preventing unauthorized access.

Authentication: The process of verifying the identity of a user, device, or system attempting to access a resource or system.

Authorization: The process of granting or denying access privileges to users or systems based on their authenticated identity and assigned permissions.

Confidentiality: The property of data or information being protected from unauthorized access or disclosure.

Integrity: The property of data or information being protected from unauthorized modification, deletion, or alteration.

NIST SP 800-53: The National Institute of Standards and Technology (NIST) Special Publication (SP) 800-53 is a framework that provides a comprehensive set of security controls and guidelines for federal information systems and organizations.

Risk Assessment: The process of identifying, analyzing, and evaluating potential risks and vulnerabilities to determine the likelihood and impact of potential security incidents.

Security Control: A safeguard or countermeasure implemented to protect the confidentiality, integrity, and availability of information and systems.

Security Plan: A comprehensive document that outlines an organization's approach to managing and implementing security controls, including roles and responsibilities, risk assessments, and incident response procedures.

System Development Life Cycle (SDLC): A structured approach used to develop, implement, and maintain IT systems, ensuring security considerations are integrated throughout the entire lifecycle.

Threat: Any potential danger or harm that can exploit vulnerabilities in an information system, including malicious attacks, natural disasters, or human errors.

Vulnerability: A weakness or flaw in an information system, software, or hardware that can be exploited by threats, potentially leading to unauthorized access or compromise of the system.

By familiarizing yourself with these terms, you will be better equipped to navigate the complexities of NIST SP 800-53 implementation for small businesses. This glossary provides a foundation for understanding the key concepts and terminology associated with the framework, allowing you to communicate effectively, interpret guidelines accurately, and implement necessary security controls to meet compliance requirements.

Remember, mastering NIST SP 800-53 is not only crucial for compliance but also for protecting your organization's sensitive data and systems from potential threats.

Appendix B: Sample NIST SP 800-53 Compliance Checklist for Small Businesses

In this appendix, we provide you with a valuable resource to aid your journey towards NIST SP 800-53 compliance. As IT professionals working in small businesses, we understand the challenges you face in implementing the rigorous security controls outlined in the NIST Special Publication 800-53.

This checklist serves as a comprehensive tool to assist you in assessing your organization's compliance status. It covers the key areas and security controls required by NIST SP 800-53, specifically tailored to the unique needs and limitations of small businesses. By utilizing this checklist, you can ensure that your organization meets the necessary standards and safeguards against potential security threats.

The checklist is divided into s corresponding to the different families of security controls outlined in NIST SP 800-53. Each section provides a detailed list of controls, along with checkboxes to mark their implementation status. This allows you to easily track your progress and identify any gaps in compliance.

While this sample checklist provides a solid foundation for NIST SP 800-53 compliance, it is important to note that every organization's needs and circumstances may vary. Therefore, we encourage you to customize this checklist according to your specific requirements. This will ensure that it aligns with your organization's unique IT infrastructure, resources, and risk profile.

By using this sample compliance checklist as a starting point, you can streamline your compliance efforts and accelerate your journey towards NIST SP 800-53 compliance. It will serve as a valuable reference tool, helping you stay organized, track your progress, and ensure that your organization meets the necessary security standards.

Remember, achieving compliance with NIST SP 800-53 is not a one-time event; it requires ongoing effort and commitment to maintain the necessary security posture. Utilize this checklist as a roadmap to guide your compliance journey and keep your small business secure in an increasingly complex digital landscape. Note that this is a generic template, and you should customize it based on your specific business operations, systems, and risk factors.

Below is a sample NIST SP 800-53 Compliance Checklist for Small Businesses based on best practices:

Access Control (AC)

1. AC-1: Access Control Policy and Procedures
   - [ ] Develop and implement a comprehensive access control policy.
   - [ ] Establish and maintain access control procedures.

2. AC-2: Account Management
   - [ ] Assign unique user accounts.
   - [ ] Implement multi-factor authentication for privileged accounts.

3. AC-3: Access Enforcement
   - [ ] Utilize mechanisms to enforce access controls.
   - [ ] Regularly review and update access permissions.

4. AC-4: Information Flow Enforcement
   - [ ] Control information flow within the organization.
   - [ ] Implement network segmentation to prevent unauthorized access.

5. AC-5: Separation of Duties
   - [ ] Identify and document duties requiring separation.
   - [ ] Enforce separation of duties through access controls.

Security Training and Awareness (AT)

6. AT-1: Security Awareness and Training Policy and Procedures
   - [ ] Develop and implement a security awareness and training policy.
   - [ ] Establish and maintain security awareness and training procedures.

7. AT-2: Security Awareness Training
   - [ ] Provide security awareness training to employees.
   - [ ] Include security training in new employee orientation.

8. AT-3: Security Training Records
   - [ ] Maintain records of security training for employees.
   - [ ] Regularly review and update training records.

Audit and Accountability (AU)

9. AU-1: Audit and Accountability Policy and Procedures
   - [ ] Develop and implement a comprehensive audit and accountability

policy.
   - [ ] Establish and maintain audit and accountability procedures.

10. AU-2: Auditable Events
   - [ ] Define and document auditable events.
   - [ ] Enable auditing for identified events on systems.

11. AU-3: Content of Audit Records
   - [ ] Define the content of audit records.
   - [ ] Ensure audit records contain necessary information.

12. AU-4: Audit Storage Capacity
   - [ ] Allocate sufficient storage for audit logs.
   - [ ] Regularly review and manage audit log storage capacity.

Security Assessment and Authorization (CA)

13. CA-1: Security Assessment and Authorization Policy and Procedures
   - [ ] Develop and implement a robust security assessment and authorization policy.
   - [ ] Establish and maintain security assessment and authorization procedures.

14. CA-2: Security Assessments
   - [ ] Conduct security assessments of information systems.
   - [ ] Analyze assessment results and take corrective actions.

15. CA-3: Security Authorization
   - [ ] Grant security authorization based on assessment results.
   - [ ] Review and update security authorizations regularly.

Configuration Management (CM)

16. CM-1: Configuration Management Policy and Procedures
   - [ ] Develop and implement a robust configuration management policy.
   - [ ] Establish and maintain configuration management procedures.

17. CM-2: Baseline Configuration
   - [ ] Establish and document baseline configurations.
   - [ ] Regularly update and review baseline configurations.

18. CM-3: Configuration Change Control
   - [ ] Implement a systematic configuration change control process.
   - [ ] Review and approve configuration changes before implementation.

Contingency Planning (CP)

19. CP-1: Contingency Planning Policy and Procedures
   - [ ] Develop and maintain a comprehensive contingency planning policy.
   - [ ] Establish and maintain contingency planning procedures.

20. CP-2: Contingency Plan
   - [ ] Develop and maintain a contingency plan.
   - [ ] Conduct regular contingency planning exercises.

21. CP-3: Contingency Training
   - [ ] Provide training for personnel involved in contingency planning and response.
   - [ ] Conduct regular training exercises for contingency personnel.

Identification and Authentication (IA)

22. IA-1: Identification and Authentication Policy and Procedures
   - [ ] Establish and implement identification and authentication policies.
   - [ ] Regularly review and update authentication mechanisms.

23. IA-2: Identification and Authentication (Organizational Users)
   - [ ] Use multi-factor authentication for accessing sensitive information.
   - [ ] Regularly review and update authentication mechanisms.

24. IA-3: Device Identification and Authentication
   - [ ] Implement device identification and authentication mechanisms.
   - [ ] Regularly review and update device authentication mechanisms.

Incident Response (IR)

25. IR-1: Incident Response Policy and Procedures
   - [ ] Develop and implement an incident response policy.
   - [ ] Establish and maintain incident response procedures.

26. IR-2: Incident Response Training and Exercises
   - [ ] Provide incident response training to employees.
   - [ ] Conduct regular incident response exercises.

27. IR-3: Incident Response Testing and Exercises
   - [ ] Test incident response capabilities.
   - [ ] Evaluate and update incident response plans.

Maintenance (MA)

28. MA-1: System Maintenance Policy and Procedures
   - [ ] Develop and implement maintenance policies and procedures.
   - [ ] Regularly update and patch systems.

29. MA-2: Controlled Maintenance
   - [ ] Conduct maintenance activities in a secure and controlled manner.
   - [ ] Establish and implement controlled maintenance procedures.

30. MA-3: Maintenance Tools
   - [ ] Control and monitor the use of maintenance tools.
   - [ ] Regularly review and update maintenance tool usage policies.

Media Protection (MP)

31. MP-1: Media Protection Policy and Procedures
   - [ ] Develop and implement media protection policies.
   - [ ] Establish and maintain media protection procedures.

32. MP-2: Media Access
   - [ ] Control access to and use of media.
   - [ ] Regularly review and update media access controls.

33. MP-3: Media Marking
   - [ ] Mark and label media with necessary classification information.
   - [ ] Regularly review and update media marking procedures.

Physical and Environmental Protection (PE)

34. PE-1: Physical and Environmental Protection Policy and Procedures
   - [ ] Implement physical security measures to protect information systems.

- [ ] Regularly review and update physical security measures.

35. PE-2: Physical Access Authorizations
    - [ ] Control physical access authorizations.
    - [ ] Regularly review and update physical access authorization lists.

36. PE-3: Physical Access Control
    - [ ] Implement physical access controls.
    - [ ] Monitor and control physical access to information system components.

Planning (PL)

37. PL-1: Security Planning Policy and Procedures
    - [ ] Develop and maintain information security plans.
    - [ ] Align security plans with organizational goals.

38. PL-2: System Security Plan
    - [ ] Regularly review and update system security plans.
    - [ ] Ensure system security plans reflect the current security posture.

39. PL-3: System Security Plan Update
    - [ ] Update system security plans in response to changes.
    - [ ] Conduct regular reviews and updates to reflect evolving risks.

Personnel Security (PS)

40. PS-1: Personnel Security Policy and Procedures
    - [ ] Establish and implement personnel security policies.
    - [ ] Conduct background checks on employees.

41. PS-2: Position Risk Designation
   - [ ] Designate risk levels for positions based on security requirements.
   - [ ] Regularly review and update position risk designations.

42. PS-3: Personnel Screening
   - [ ] Screen personnel before granting access.
   - [ ] Conduct periodic personnel security screenings.

Risk Assessment (RA)

43. RA-1: Risk Assessment Policy and Procedures
   - [ ] Conduct regular risk assessments.
   - [ ] Identify and assess risks to information systems.

44. RA-2: Security Categorization
   - [ ] Categorize information systems based on impact levels.
   - [ ] Regularly review and update security categorizations.

45. RA-3: Risk Assessment Update
   - [ ] Update risk assessments based on changes.
   - [ ] Conduct regular reviews and updates to reflect evolving risks.

Security Assessment (SA)

46. SA-1: Security Assessment Policy and Procedures
   - [ ] Establish and implement security assessment policies.
   - [ ] Conduct security assessments of information systems.

47. SA-2: Security Assessment Plan
   - [ ] Develop and maintain a security assessment plan.
   - [ ] Regularly review and update the security assessment plan.

48. SA-3: Security Assessment Report
   - [ ] Generate and maintain security assessment reports.
   - [ ] Share assessment results with relevant stakeholders.

System and Communications Protection (SC)

49. SC-1: System and Communications Protection Policy and Procedures
   - [ ] Implement security controls to protect communication channels.
   - [ ] Monitor and control communication at system boundaries.

50. SC-2: Application Partitioning
   - [ ] Partition applications to prevent unauthorized access.
   - [ ] Regularly review and update application partitioning controls.

51. SC-3: Security Function Isolation
   - [ ] Isolate security functions to prevent unauthorized access.
   - [ ] Regularly review and update security function isolation measures.

System and Information Integrity (SI)

52. SI-1: System and Information Integrity Policy and Procedures
   - [ ] Implement measures to detect and prevent system and information integrity violations.
   - [ ] Regularly monitor and respond to security events.

53. SI-2: Flaw Remediation
   - [ ] Identify and remediate system flaws promptly.
   - [ ] Regularly review and update flaw remediation procedures.

54. SI-3: Malicious Code Protection
   - [ ] Implement protection measures against malicious code.

- [ ] Regularly update and review malicious code protection controls.

Program Management (PM)

55. PM-1: Program Management Policy and Procedures
   - [ ] Develop and implement information security programs.
   - [ ] Establish and maintain program management policies and procedures.

56. PM-2: Program Management Controls
   - [ ] Regularly review and update program management practices.
   - [ ] Ensure alignment of security programs with organizational goals.

57. PM-3: Program Management Update
   - [ ] Update program management practices based on changes.
   - [ ] Conduct regular reviews and updates to reflect evolving risks.

This checklist provides a comprehensive overview of the NIST SP 800-53 control families for small businesses. Customize each control based on the specific needs and context of your organization. Regular reviews and updates are essential to address evolving risks and ensure ongoing compliance.

This checklist covers all 18 control families outlined in NIST SP 800-53 and serves as a foundation for small businesses to assess and improve their security posture. Tailor each control based on the specific needs and context of your organization. Regular reviews and updates are essential to address evolving risks and ensure ongoing compliance.

In conclusion, this appendix provides you with a sample NIST SP 800-53 compliance checklist designed specifically for small businesses. It empowers you as an IT professional to navigate the implementation process effectively, ensuring that your organization meets the required security controls and safeguards.

Appendix C: Additional Resources and References for Small Business IT Professionals

As an IT professional working in small businesses, understanding and implementing NIST SP 800-53 compliance can be a daunting task. However, with the right resources and references at your disposal, you can navigate this complex landscape and ensure your organization meets the necessary security standards. In this appendix, we have compiled a comprehensive list of additional resources to assist you in your journey towards NIST SP 800-53 compliance.

1. **NIST Special Publications:** The National Institute of Standards and Technology (NIST) offers a wide range of special publications that provide detailed guidance on various aspects of information security. These publications are invaluable resources for small business IT professionals looking to understand and implement NIST SP 800-53 controls effectively.

2. **NIST Cybersecurity Framework:** The NIST Cybersecurity Framework provides a structured approach to managing cybersecurity risk. It outlines a set of core functions, categories, and subcategories that can help small businesses align their security practices with industry best

practices.

3. NIST Risk Management Framework: The NIST Risk Management Framework (RMF) provides a structured approach to managing cybersecurity risk within federal organizations. Small businesses can adapt this framework to their specific needs and use it as a guide for implementing NIST SP 800-53 controls.

4. NIST SP 800-171: While NIST SP 800-53 focuses on federal systems, NIST SP 800-171 specifically addresses the protection of controlled unclassified information (CUI) in non-federal systems. Small businesses that handle CUI can benefit from referencing this publication alongside NIST SP 800-53.

5. Small Business Administration (SBA) Resources: The SBA provides numerous resources and tools tailored specifically for small businesses. These resources cover a wide range of topics, including cybersecurity best practices, risk management, and compliance guidelines.

6. Industry-specific Associations: Many industries have associations that offer specialized resources and guidance on IT security. For example, the Healthcare Information and Management Systems Society (HIMSS) provides resources specifically for IT professionals in the healthcare sector. Identifying and engaging with these associations can provide sector-specific insights and support.

7. Online Communities and Forums: Engaging with online communities and forums dedicated to NIST SP 800-53 implementation for small businesses can be incredibly valuable. These platforms provide opportunities to connect with other IT professionals facing similar challenges, share experiences, and seek advice.

Remember, compliance with NIST SP 800-53 is an ongoing process, and it requires continuous monitoring and improvement. By utilizing the resources and references mentioned above, you can stay up to date with the latest guidelines, best practices, and tools that will aid you in effectively implementing and maintaining NIST SP 800-53 controls within your small business.

In conclusion, this appendix serves as a valuable compilation of additional resources and references specifically tailored to small business IT professionals navigating the complexities of NIST SP 800-53 compliance. By leveraging these resources, you can streamline your compliance efforts, enhance your organization's security posture, and ultimately safeguard your small business against evolving cyber threats.

www.ingramcontent.com/pod-product-compliance
Lightning Source LLC
Chambersburg PA
CBHW050034260726
48658CB00005B/1592